# How Mumm[y and] Mama Made a Baby

## Conceived with IVF

### Written and illustrated
### by Emma Wallis

Published in the UK by Emma Wallis—January 2018

ISBN: 9781976967177

Visit Emma's page: fb.me/EmmaWallisAuthor

For Teddy

This is the story of mummy and mama.

# Mama works in an office.

# Mummy works in a library.

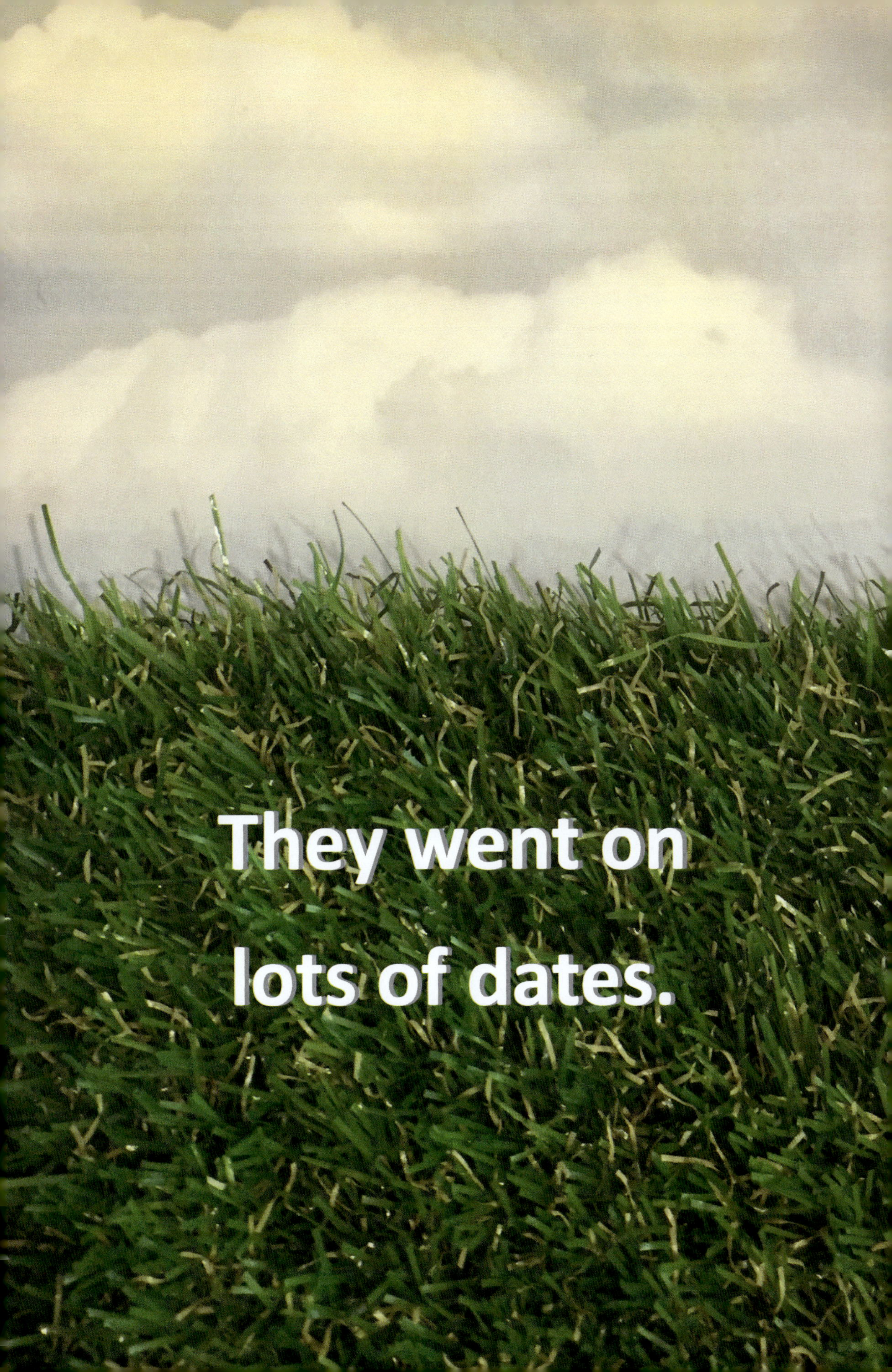

They went on lots of dates.

# They went out to dinner.

# And to the theatre.

# They went on lots of adventures together.

They found new hobbies, like camping.

# Mummy taught mama how to cook...

... and how to bake.

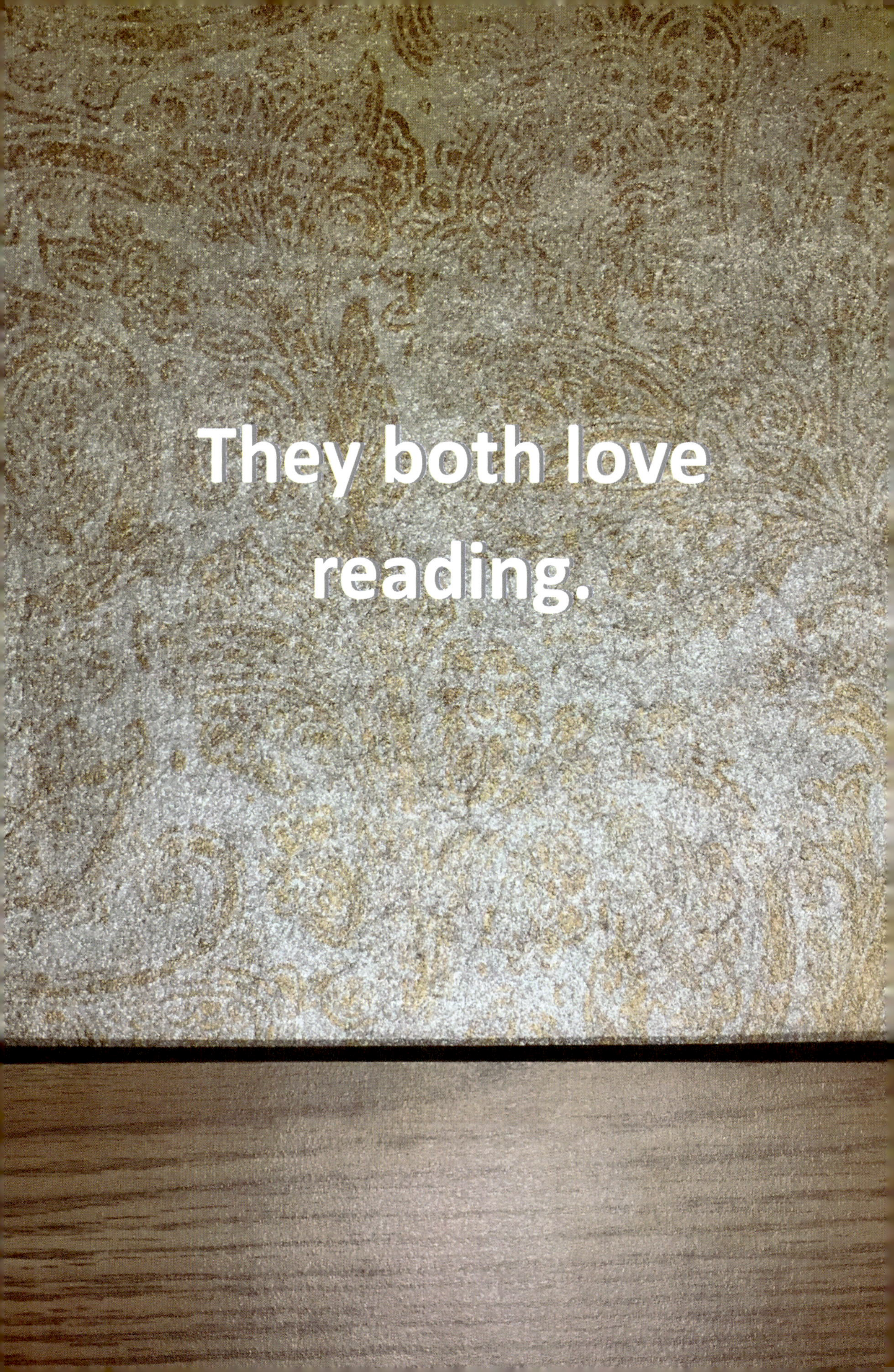
They both love
reading.

# They wanted to be a family.

# They went on honeymoon!

# They decided to have a baby.

# Reproduction is a type of sex.

Sex can be between adults of any gender and it is not just to make a baby.

Sometimes adults have sex just because it feels nice. This is why same sex couples have sex.

They are both women. This is called a same sex relationship.

# A fertility clinic helps people have babies.

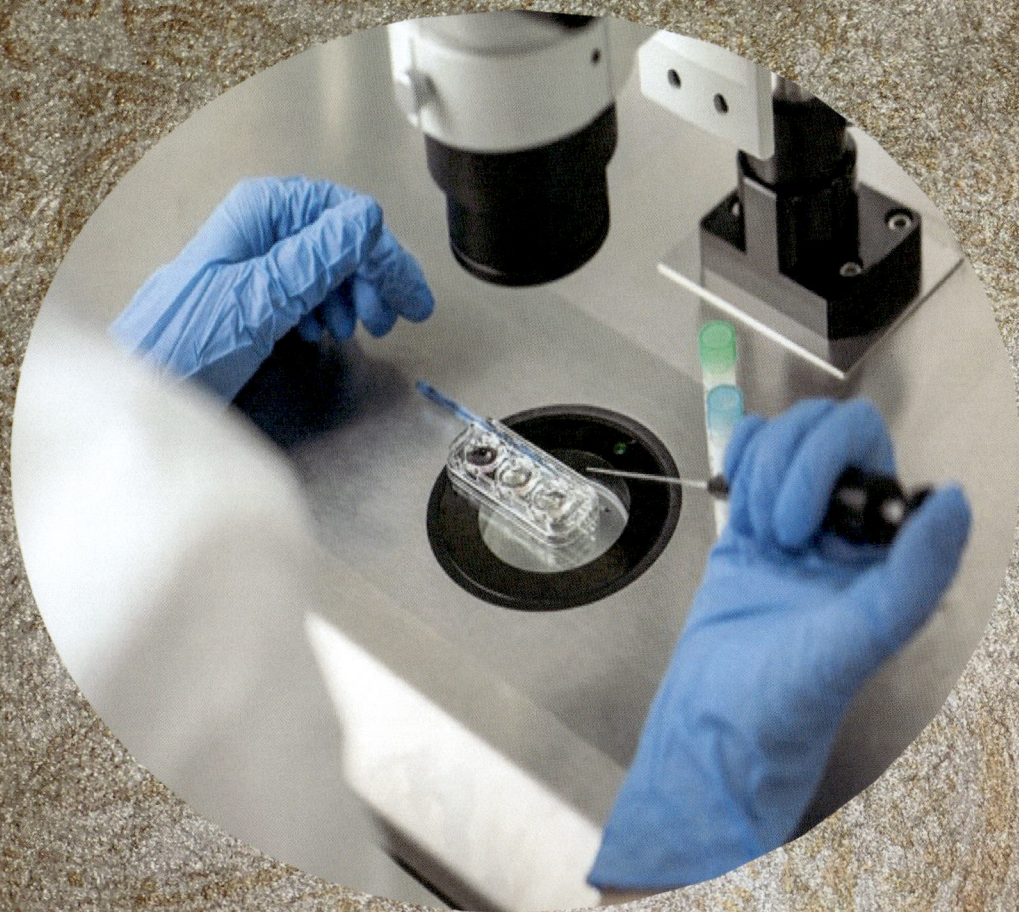

A man called a sperm donor donated some of his sperm to the sperm bank.

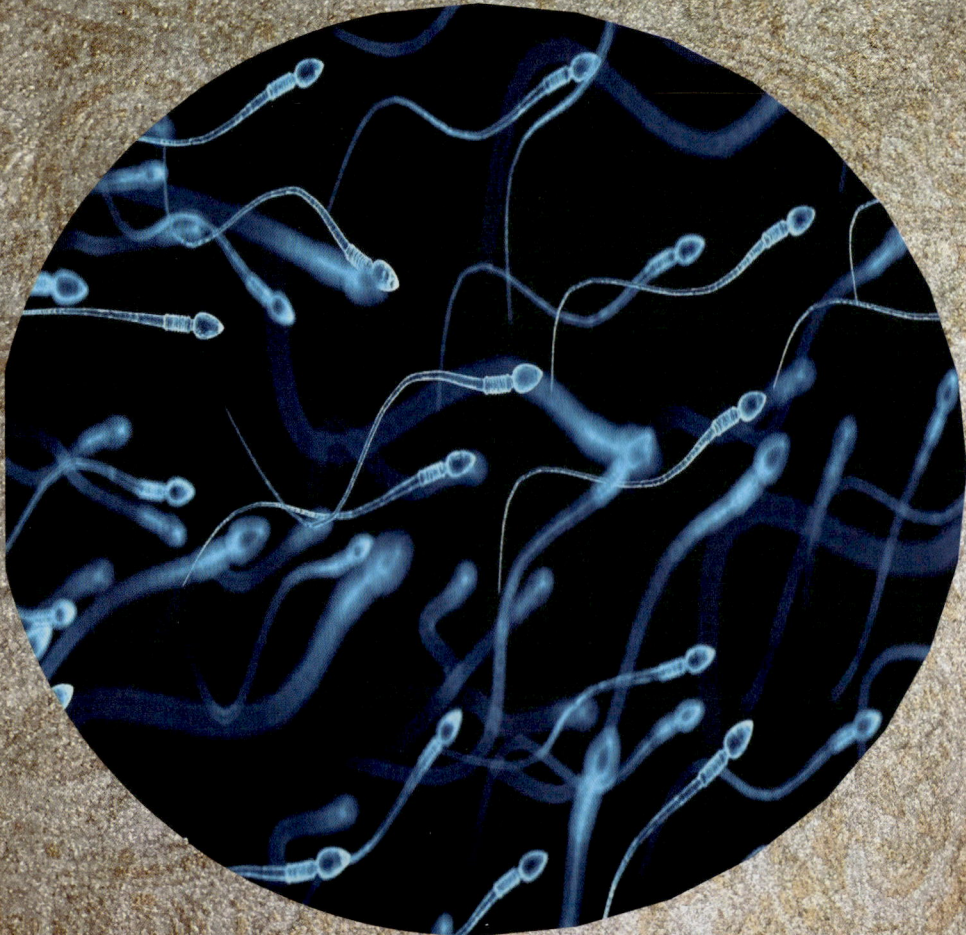

# The fertility doctor collected some eggs from Mummy.

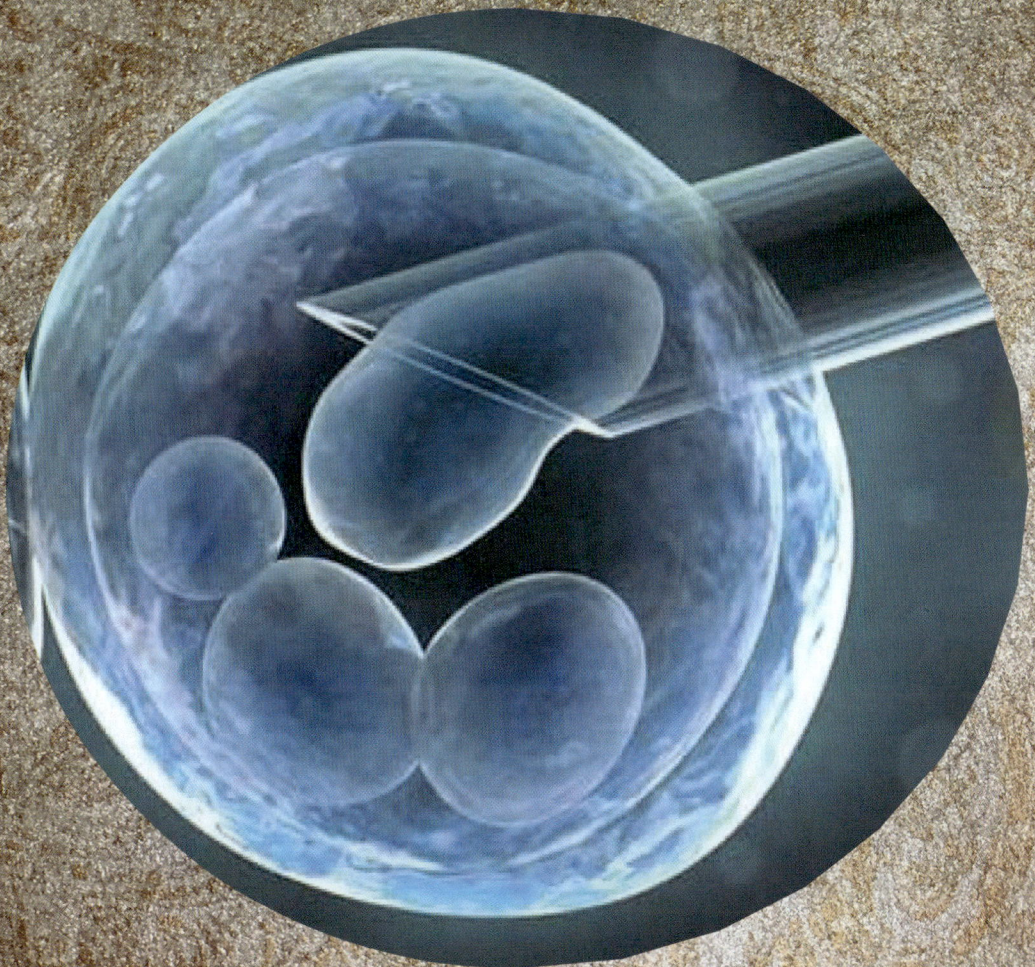

The fertility doctor introduced the sperm to the egg. This is called fertilisation.

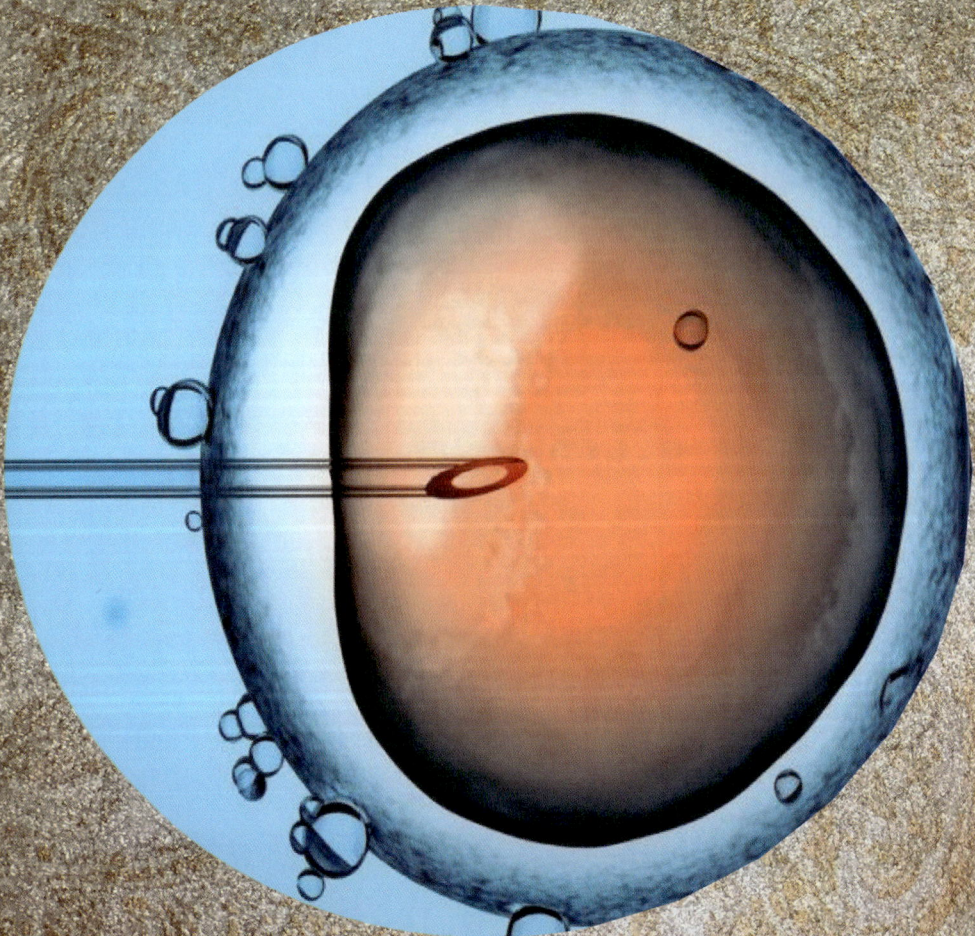

# The fertilised egg is called an embryo. The doctor put the embryo back into Mummy's tummy.

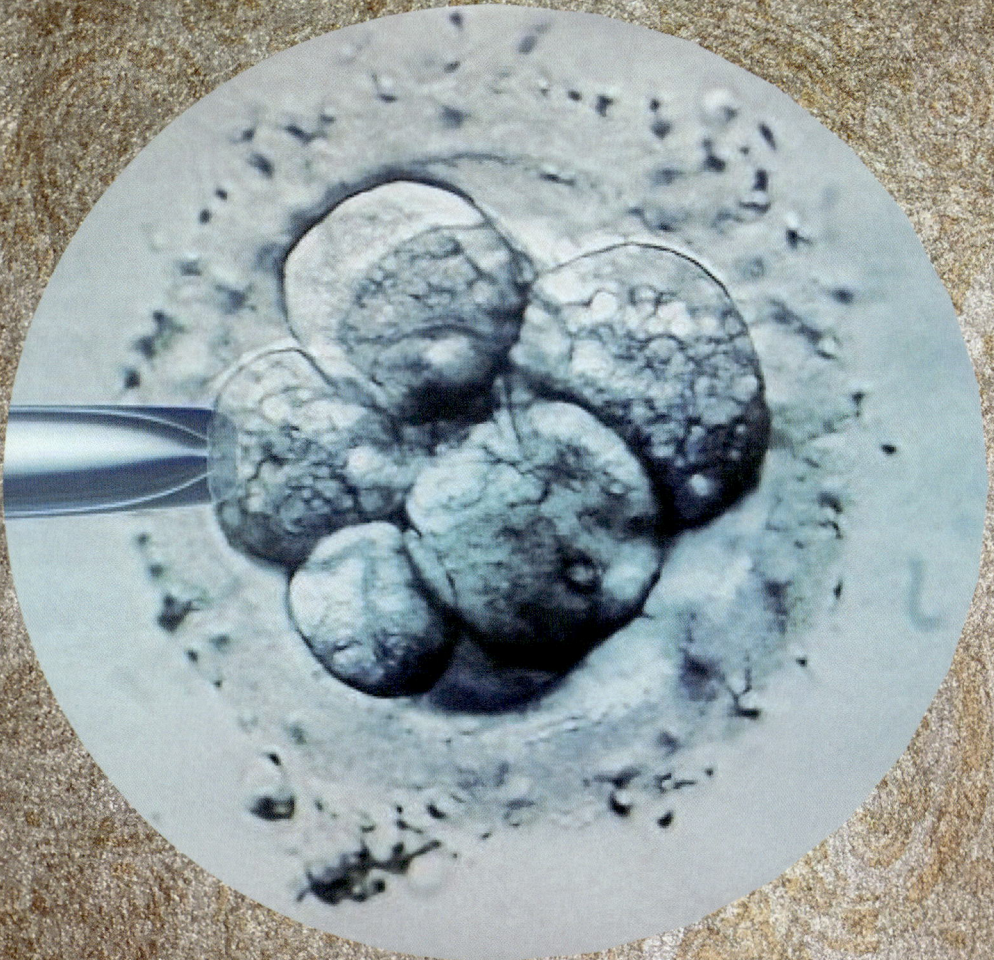

# The embryo started to form a baby...

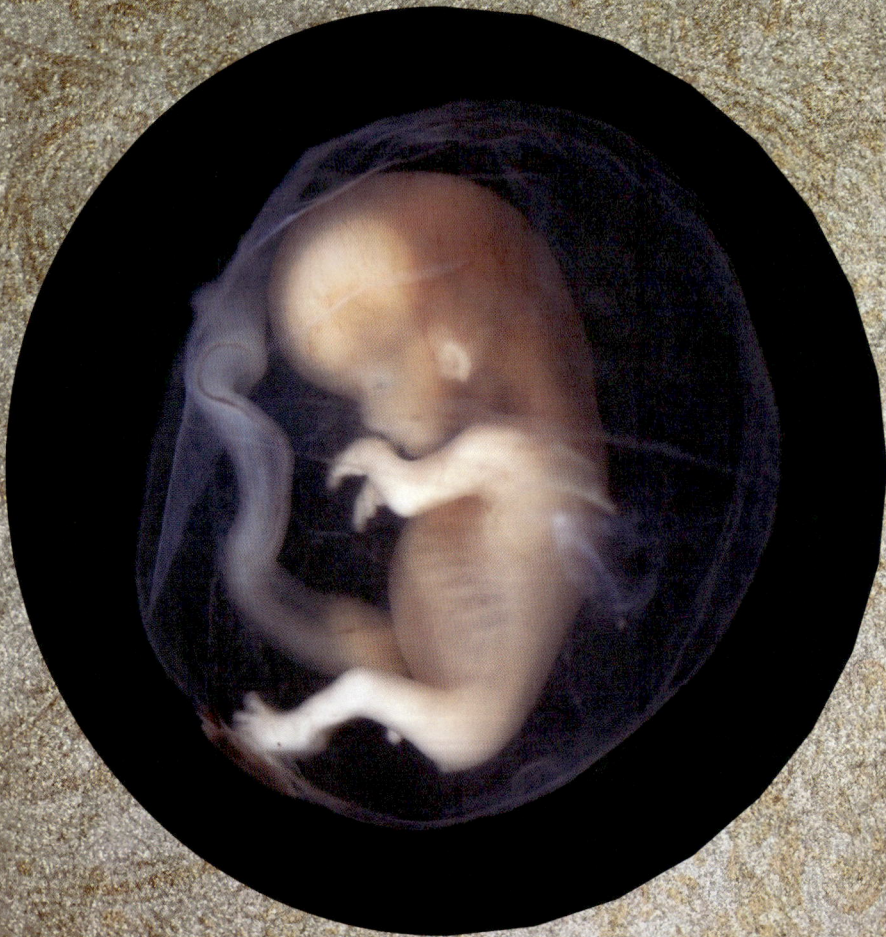

# ... and the baby grew!

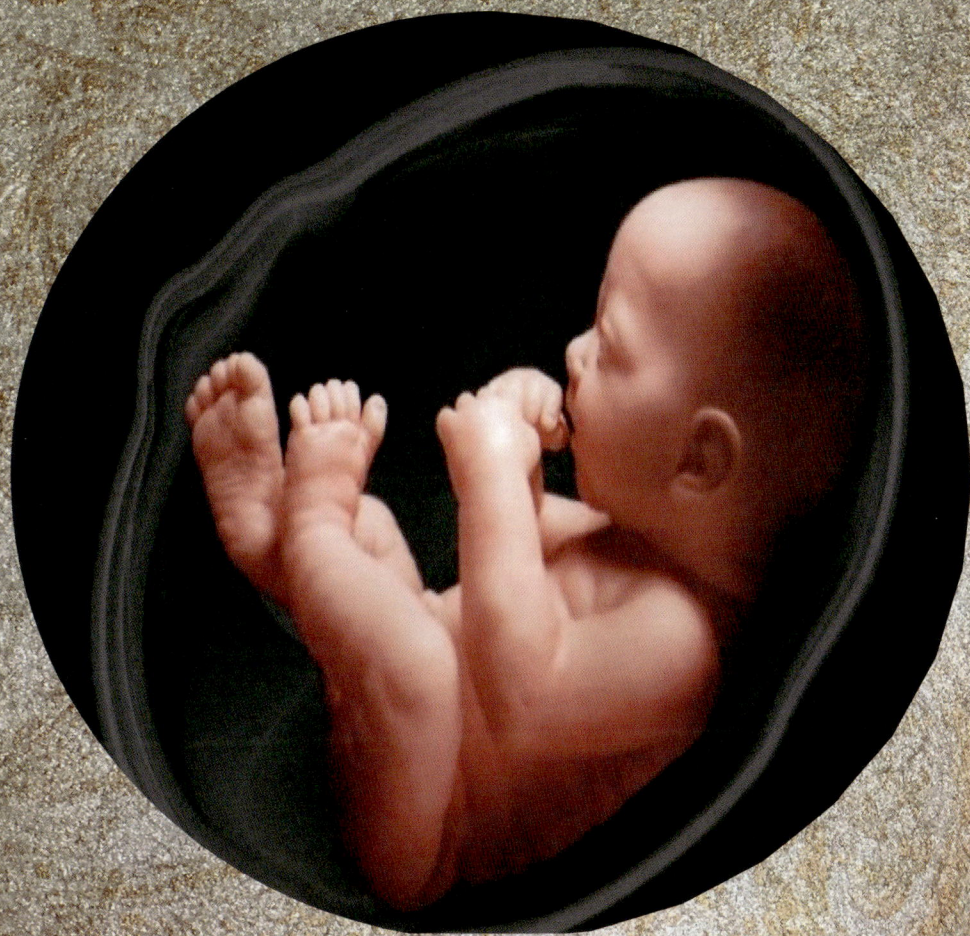

# After nine months in mummy's tummy, their baby was born!